"Meditation is the cornerstone of spiritual awakening; it is a time of listening to one's spiritual information... Meditation is a quieting of the mind-body system and an opening of the spiritual system... As you turn within during meditation, you learn to see yourself as the one who decides your fate."

BOOKS BY MARY ELLEN FLORA

The *Key Series*:

> **Meditation**: Key to Spiritual Awakening
> **Healing**: Key to Spiritual Balance
> **Clairvoyance**: Key to Spiritual Perspective
> **Chakras**: Key to Spiritual Opening

It is recommended that you read the *Key Series* in the order indicated above. Each book acts as a spiritual textbook to provide a foundation in basic spiritual techniques which helps you prepare, on a level of spiritual awareness, for the next book. All of the material is of a spiritual nature. Allow a spiritual perspective and you will benefit from the information. You must practice the techniques for them to work for you because you cannot intellectualize spiritual information.

The *Energy Series*:

> **Cosmic Energy**: The Creative Power
> **Earth Energy**: The Spiritual Frontier
> **Male and Female Energies**: The Balancing Act
> **Kundalini Energy**: The Flame of Life

MEDITATION

Key to Spiritual Awakening

Second Edition

by Mary Ellen Flora

CDM Publications   Everett, Washington

Cover Art: Carrie Harris

Illustrations: Carrie Harris, Jeff Gibson, and Johanna Stark

Cover Photography: The Everett Photo Shoppe

Requests for such permission should be addressed to:

CDM Publications
2402 Summit Avenue
Everett, WA 98201

First Edition 1991.
Second Edition 2000.

Library of Congress Cataloging-in-Publication Data

Flora, Mary Ellen.
    Meditation : key to spiritual awakening / by Mary Ellen Flora.-- 2nd ed.
        p. cm.
    Includes index.
    ISBN 1-886983-11-9 (pbk. : alk.paper)
    1. Meditation.   I. Title.

BL627 .F54 2000
291.4'35--dc21

                                                            00-025848

Printed on recycled paper in the United States of America.
Malloy Lithographing Inc., Ann Arbor, Michigan

THIS BOOK IS DEDICATED TO
M. F. "DOC" SLUSHER
WHO HAS MADE
MEDITATION
HIS WAY OF LIFE.

TABLE OF CONTENTS

ACKNOWLEDGEMENTS

Many thanks to all who have helped with the second expanded edition of this book. Special thanks to Carrie Harris for her excellent graphic art for the cover and diagrams. Thank you to Jeff Gibson and Johanna Stark for their artwork.

I greatly appreciate the work and support of Melissa Carmichael as our production leader. Many thanks to Kim Zirbes for her physical and spiritual support. Special thanks to Diane Brewster for leading the administrative team and constantly encouraging everyone, including me.

Lembi Kongas has been a support in this book as in previous ones, and her editing and proofreading skills are a gift to the whole team. Thanks also goes to Sara Canady and Jo Ann Newton for their proofreading. Much appreciation goes to Jeff Rice for his work on the index.

Continued appreciation to those who helped produce the first book, which is the foundation of this edition, especially Bill Broomall, Sharon Haywood, Alison Eckels, Tom Eckels, and Nancy Weymouth. Also, warm appreciation goes to Lewis Bostwick who introduced me to meditation.

Most of all, I wish to express my love and gratitude to M. F. "Doc" Slusher who has taught me to be strong enough to follow my path.

INTRODUCTION

For many years, I have taught classes focused on spiritual awakening. During that time, I have learned that, more than anything else, people need to learn to meditate. All of the answers to our questions are within us. What remains for us to do is to find a way to turn within for our unique information and our internal path to God. Meditation is the way within to spiritual awakening and the realization that our spiritual guidance is essential for us to create what we need. Because the Creator of all things, or All That Is, or Cosmic Consciousness, or whatever name you use, really has no name, throughout this book I will most often refer to our Divine Source as God.

People have asked me so many times, in so many ways, "How do I find my information to solve my problems?" My reply is always, "Learn to meditate." When you learn to meditate, you begin to remember how to tune in to your spiritual self and, thus, how to tune in to God. All of the answers to your questions can be found within yourself. When you look within, you find the divine spark of God within you. This God Consciousness provides all of the information you seek.

Meditation leads you into yourself as it involves quieting the physical and focusing on the spiritual. Meditation is the only way I know to truly find the answers to your life questions. With meditation, you put your attention back on the spiritual realm within and seek your information there instead of looking outside yourself for your answers in the physical world around you.

I believe that most people have discovered that a new car, a new outfit, a vacation or any other physical acquisition or action will not solve a problem, other than on a superficial level that is not lasting. We also need to realize that our information is found within ourselves and not in the world around us. To solve the major problems or answer the important questions of life, we need our spiritual guidance which is found within. With only the physical perspective, we continue to create the same problems over and over because we focus outside and do not listen to the spiritual answers within.

One young man I know has been asking me the same questions for several years and refuses to hear that he needs to meditate to get to know himself. He continues to create disastrous relationships and to fight with the women in his life. He is so focused on things outside of himself that he is nervous, confused and unhappy.

By meditating, he could find the beliefs within himself that keep him caught in this destructive pattern. Through continued meditation, he could clear those old concepts and debilitating patterns. Fortunately, God sent him a daughter to teach him, as he refuses to help himself.

There are many examples of people who have used meditation successfully. One young woman called from the East Coast, in a state of fear and despair. She was afraid of not being able to live up to the expectations of others. Her fear of needing to please others had become so intense it had engulfed her life. She was unable to enjoy her marriage, job, friends or herself in any way. The expectations and fear had become a barrier to her spiritual communication like a veil of darkness in which she felt alone and lost. Meditation was her way out of the darkness of unawareness. By using the techniques, she was able to take back control of her life. At this time, she is learning to like herself as the bright being she is instead of trying to be what she thought others wanted her to be.

A woman who took a meditation class from a teacher used the techniques to help her clear hate from her body. The intensity of that emotion had created a physical illness in her body. She used meditation to turn within, cleanse herself of the harmful energy and cure the illness.

Whether you have a teacher or use the book to assist you in teaching yourself how to meditate, the results can be the same. You can become aware that you are spirit with a body through which you create. You are the creator of your reality. Meditation can help you regain conscious control of your creations. You will eventually be able to communicate with your higher spiritual self and your God.

I hope this book of simple instruction on how to meditate will help many who are asking the same question about how to get back in touch with themselves and their own answers. Many people call me from various parts of the U.S., Canada, Europe and Australia asking for assistance in their life creations. This book is for those who do not have access to a teacher to help them as well as for those who want a refresher on the techniques. The simple techniques presented can help anyone who uses them to create a meditative state to receive his or her own spiritual information.

My prayer is that all of you who read this simple book will use it to bring the bright light of God into your life. Once this light is within you, it will also bring light to everything around you.

MEDITATION

Meditation is the cornerstone of spiritual awakening; it is a time of listening to one's spiritual information. You meditate when you sit quietly and silence the distractions of the physical world in order to hear a message from the spiritual realm. Meditation is a quieting of the mind-body system and an opening of the spiritual system. The purpose of meditation is to communicate with the Cosmic Consciousness or God.

This ultimate purpose of meditating, to re-establish your one-to-one communication with God, takes you on a journey of getting to know yourself and your creations. As you turn within during meditation, you find your path to God within you. You learn to see yourself as the creator of your reality and the one who decides your fate. You realize that each lifetime offers learning opportunities, and meditation can help you use each life to the fullest. If you do not focus on your spiritual lesson, you will return again and again in other lives until you learn that lesson. Like the young man in the introduction who refuses to solve his problems and continues to blame others for his creations, you will repeat your mistakes until you stop and listen to your spiritual self and God.

As each individual meditates, communication with God is enhanced for all of humanity. When you create your life from your spiritual information rather than from your physical desires, you raise your awareness and the awareness of all those with whom you come in contact. Meditation is the process through which you can heal yourself and your world. It is the path back to your spiritual awareness and your open relationship with God.

Meditation is not as familiar to most people as prayer. Prayer is most often used to ask for something and to thank God for what we have received. We have all used prayer at some time in our lives, sometimes without being consciously aware of it. We have prayed to have someone we love healed, asked to have our burden of despair lifted, prayed for answers to our questions. Even a wish is a form of prayer since it asks an unknown source for something; so everyone has prayed in one form or another. Almost everyone has thanked God for something, either out of heartfelt gratitude or from relief.

One problem most people have with prayer is that they are often so busy asking that they forget to listen for the answer. This unwillingness to listen is one reason our prayers often seem to go unanswered. The answers are, in fact, given to us, and we only need to be quiet and listen to hear them. Too often, we behave like children asking, "Why? Why?" and not listening to the answer the adult is attempting to give. Meditation is the time of listening. It is the time to hear the answers to our prayers and much more.

Throughout the ages, human beings have sought communication with God for various reasons, ranging from despair over the chaos of the world to the desire to rejoice in the beauty within and around us. A daily communication with God, or meditation time, allows us to have this spiritual interaction. People in most cultures set aside a time of quiet worship during their day. Native Americans traditionally have welcomed the sun and the new day with a morning meditation. Moslems heed their daily calls to prayer. Christians have their daily devotionals. Buddhists meditate each day. An investigation into a variety of religions and cultures will reveal that most of them encourage regular meditation in some form. The human race long has recognized this essential need for communication with our Creator.

As we reopen our awareness to the need for this quiet period during our day, we discover that this communication with God is available to us at all times and in all places. We learn that we do not need an intermediary to intercede with God for us, a special place that is more sacred than others or a sacrifice to appease God. We do not need anything except ourselves and the ever-present Cosmic Consciousness.

In God we are one. We have divided ourselves into bodies to learn and grow. In our division, we created varied religions to help us reunite ourselves with God. The different religions all have basically the same purpose: a system for seeking and communicating with God. Unfortunately, we have gotten lost in the superficial differences and have forgotten the essential truth that we are all united as one in God.

Our meditations allow us to open to the awareness of our individual oneness with God and the oneness of all things in God. Meditation helps us see our ultimate oneness regardless of the path we take. There are as many paths to God as there are souls, and our personal meditation leads us within to our path.

Since meditation is spiritual communication, it is necessary for us to believe that we are spiritual beings in order for it to be effective. We become more aware of ourselves as spirit as we practice meditation. Just as musicians practice their music or athletes exercise and train for their sport, one must practice meditation to develop proficiency. The more we meditate, the more capable we become in our spiritual communication. We also gain more awareness of others as spirit as we learn more about ourselves as spirit. We realize that each of us is not just a body, but a spiritual being residing in a body.

Many people on this planet Earth have forgotten that we are spirit and not just the body. So many ask, "Who am I?" A simple answer is that we are spirit; each of us is a spark of God manifesting in a physical body to learn how to experience and express God on a new level of awareness. We are in this physical reality to develop spiritually, but we have forgotten that we are spirit and why we are here. Because we have become so enamored with our physical experience, we have lost touch with our spirituality and original purpose. It is necessary for us to learn to meditate to get back in touch with our true selves, our spiritual selves.

One example of the benefit of meditation is a student who had an extremely disturbing childhood filled with abuse, pain and fear. She had forgotten who she was when she arrived at our healing center. It took her over a year of focused meditation for her to recognize her spiritual nature. It required patience from her teachers and commitment from her to move her awareness from a survival level to a spiritual level. When she regained her spiritual perspective, she began to create as spirit. She relearned to be in charge of her survival needs and created a place to live and a job. She even began to experience her joy and enthusiasm. She eventually regained her awareness of herself as a spiritual healer and helped other people with similar life experiences.

We have allowed our physical creations and ego to become more important to us than spirit. We have engulfed ourselves with limiting beliefs, and have ceased to recognize ourselves as spirit. The more we identify with the limits we have created in the physical world, the more we feel overpowered by them. We begin to doubt our spiritual origin and abilities. We begin to fight this sense of helplessness and loneliness. The more we struggle against our own self-created web of darkness or unawareness, the more we become entwined within it. We become like the woman who lost her spiritual awareness so thoroughly she could no longer care for her physical needs because she was so focused on her pain, fear and limits. We forget that we simply need to acknowledge our spiritual light and our communication with God to rekindle the spiritual flame within. When we light the spark and communicate as spirit, the darkness of unawareness melts away.

Every person is a spiritual being and is here on this Earth to learn unique lessons. Each of us has created individual lessons to learn with the guidance of God. Since we need to learn so many things, we have the God-given experiences of time and space, reincarnation and other ways to allow a process for our growth. Reincarnation, the illusion of time and space and the veil of the physical world are all part of this opportunity to make mistakes and overcome our mistakes in order to learn and grow spiritually. God has also given us all freedom to choose to return to our Creator of our own free will. We need time and opportunities to find our personal way back to God. As spirit, we are like children learning and growing through the creativity of our life.

We choose to mature through our lessons or to remain separate from our mature spiritual state. Through these lessons, the development of our spiritual maturity brings us back to God.

When we complete our lessons here on Earth, each one of us is able to become an enlightened being such as Jesus Christ, Buddha, Lao Tsu, Mohammed and the many other great spiritual teachers both known and unknown. We can attune ourselves to God, as they did, by cleansing and clearing the physical barriers we create, such as fear, hate and doubt. By taking charge of the body's desires and using all of our energies to communicate with God, we begin our return to our Source. By awakening to the reality that we are spirit and clearing away the veil of physical illusion, we can communicate with God as our teachers have. They meditated to experience this communication, and so must we.

All spirit seeks communication, so you will soon come to enjoy the quiet communion meditation brings, if you persevere. Meditation allows your awareness of yourself and all others as spirit, and helps you to see and express your spiritual path on earth. It helps you gain and maintain your spiritual perspective. Meditation assists you to transform your physical reality to your spiritual purpose.

Everyone is a part of God. God created us from powers beyond our comprehension. We were created to manifest an aspect of God called love. We were given free will in order to make this wonderful manifestation possible. This freedom is necessary because we must love God above all things and return to God of our own free choice. Meditation brings us the spiritual awareness necessary to master the will of our body and the pull of our physical creations so that we desire this spiritual unity above all else.

The freedom we have been given offers great challenge as it has a detrimental aspect as well. With our free will, we can also destroy the infinite possibilities of our creative challenge by choosing to move away from God. We can use our freedom to create doubt and to separate ourselves from God instead of using it to bring ourselves closer to our Creator. We choose every moment of every day to move toward or away from God. We choose to be kind or mean, afraid or loving, enthusiastic or depressed. We all do a dance of toward and away, hopefully always choosing enough of the higher energy creative levels to eventually return our focus to God.

In our creative immaturity, we doubt that there is anything beyond ourselves. We doubt the very existence of God; thus, we stop listening to the guidance from the Cosmic Consciousness. We become more and more lost in our physical world and forget the spiritual realm. We lose touch with God's purpose for us and create from the desires of the body and the demands of the ego. We use our freedom to create what we think we want instead of what we are meant to create. We forget that freedom of will is given to us so we can freely return to God of our own choice.

Meditation is a path back to the level of spiritual awareness that allows us to seek a return to God. When we meditate, we hear what we need to do as spirit. We begin to open ourselves to the spiritual world we have forgotten. By sitting still and listening, we hear the will of God and awaken our desire to return to our Source. We also heal and change the body to be used for our spiritual purpose. We learn to make this journey through the vibration of love that God has created us to manifest.

There are many forms of meditation on this Earth. There are meditations to assist the soul to be more in tune with the body and some to assist the soul to be separate from the body. There is no perfect form of meditation; however, there is a meditation which is correct for each individual soul according to its present growth. Planet Earth is a reality filled with opposites and a place for us to learn balance. The type of meditation presented in this book is one of balance. It includes an awareness of both spirit and body.

One goal of beneficial meditation is to learn to balance spirit and body. Since the purpose of meditation is to re-establish one's communication with God, we need to be aware that the body is our communication system in the physical world. As we connect the body to the rest of physical reality, we connect ourselves, as spirit, through our communication system, the body, to our chosen learning medium, the planet, which is our larger collective body. When we do this, we learn that we need to clear from our body all foreign and debilitating energies in order to communicate most clearly through it. The clearer the medium, the clearer the message.

This process of cleansing through meditation takes time and space as do all things in this physical reality. When we begin cleansing, we discover the energy and information of our parents, siblings, friends, teachers, children, enemies and all with whom we have interacted during this lifetime. We also discover inappropriate concepts we have accepted from others, created ourselves and brought forward from past lives. Other things we have stored in the body which we must cleanse are debilitating energies such as pain, doubt, hate, criticism, judgement, guilt and grief.

This list of cleansing projects may seem insurmountable; however, you do have an entire lifetime to work on healing yourself. Also, all during this journey, you will be communicating with God. This enhances your clarity, so your cleansing or healing becomes easier with every passing day of meditation. The important thing is to continue with your meditation and not be discouraged when you discover another project. Like all things in the physical realm, meditation requires time and attention.

These times of communication with God during meditation assist you to pass through the difficult learning experiences of life and to fully enjoy the joyous times. Whether the lesson relates to a creation in present time, the clearing of past experiences or the cleansing of foreign energies, the quiet time spent in communion with God gives you the strength to continue your spiritual path.

Many give up meditation practices after a short time, as they are disappointed by the results. They begin to experience all the disturbing or painful energies they have created and allowed in their reality, and stop meditating before they work through the difficulties. Many people expect meditation to bring instant pleasure, immediate peace and enlightenment. They forget that they have been filling their bodies and lives with pain and problems for many years.

Unrealistic expectations stop us from experiencing what exists in our reality. When we do accept what we have created, we can change whatever we need to change. We can heal ourselves and create what we want in the present instead of continuing to create with past time and inappropriate concepts. We can learn to find joy in our present experiences, including meditation, when we accept ourselves as we are. Only then can we progress.

Several years ago, a member of my staff complained to me about having to meditate every day and clear her spiritual system regularly. I asked if she had any judgement about washing her hands or bathing. I hoped the humor of the question would help her cease to take herself so seriously. She missed the amusement and in anger replied, "Of course not." I pointed out that cleansing your spiritual system is necessary to operate as spirit in the body just as cleansing your body is needed to operate in most societies. I reminded her that spiritual work requires focus and commitment. Unfortunately, she lacked both of these characteristics and so left the spiritual path for a physical focus.

A friend of mine had a different experience with meditation. He found that he was uncomfortable if he did not meditate. He started on his spiritual journey with enthusiasm and then allowed his business to sidetrack him from his spiritual focus. He became more and more disturbed and frightened as he meditated less. After six months, he returned to his spiritual community and resumed his meditations and healing focus. His work, as well as the other aspects of his life, improved as he again meditated regularly and used his spiritual abilities along with his physical skills. His previous joy with meditation gave him a light to follow and return to when he got off track for awhile.

Not accepting the body as it is also interferes with your spiritual awakening and creativity. Since you use your body when you meditate, you need to respect it and its characteristics. Spirit and body are opposite, and you need to accept and love both as they are to balance your spirit-body experience. Spirit is immortal. It is not bound by time, space, mass, emotions, effort, competition or ethics. The body is mortal. It operates through time, space, mass, emotions, effort, competition and ethics. You need to know and accept these differences so you, as spirit, can work with your body and not expect it to be like you.

Because your body functions in time and space, anything you, as spirit, do takes time for the body to process and learn. Meditation practices require time to learn and use since you are using your body as the meditation tool. You can teach your body to respond to you and be less affected by its emotions, effort and other characteristics if you commit to your meditation time.

When you have broken through the clouds just once and have experienced the beauty of communication and oneness through meditating, the process becomes so meaningful that it is difficult to eliminate from your life. You begin to enjoy your body and your body begins to welcome you. This takes time and patience, and it is well worth the time and energy invested.

The main ingredient to assure continued meditation practices is commitment to the process. It is not necessary to be intelligent, talented, good, pure or anything else. You must simply be committed enough to continue your focus on meditation until you reach a level of spiritual awareness that will carry you onward. This means working through the doubt, fear and pain you have stored in your body so you can fill it with your own spiritual energy. Meditation is similar to physical exercise as there are highs and lows and plateaus in your progress. When you persevere through the lows and plateaus, you achieve your goals. The debilitating energies mentioned act as a barrier between you and God and between you and all others. When you clear them and fill your body with your unique spiritual energy, you open your spiritual communication channels. You experience your oneness with all things.

Since meditation brings a new level of awareness, the process takes time and attention. Being quiet takes perseverance, and meditation requires being quiet. The spirit needs to re-establish its seniority over the body and relearn how to communicate through its body. The body needs to learn to accept the spirit and to be cleansed of the inappropriate information the spirit has stored within it. This spirit-body relationship is essential to our clear communication. We have to cleanse the ego we have created. The ego is composed of doubt, pain, fear, hate and any other misery which we have stored in the body and covered with the facade that says the misery does not exist. When this facade is cleared, or even in the process of clearing, our communication opens. We become aware that we are spirit; the body is our creation for learning and communication; and our source and life is God.

Meditation takes on new meaning when we realize that it is our bridge back to God. It not only helps us raise our own vibration so that we can heal ourselves, it also assists others. By meditating, we raise the vibration of everything within and around us. Whatever exists within the individual also exists in the world. The world is our mutual creation; so when we heal ourselves, we heal everything around us. Our healing ripples out from us and affects those close to us, which affects others, and so on, as it ripples forth through the Earth.

We can think of our meditations as a way to cleanse the garbage we have all helped to create so we can communicate clearly again as spirit. We are like a group of people who has dumped its garbage in the same place in the sea for so long that the garbage has mutated into a living, growing organism. That living garbage then begins to threaten the well-being and even the existence of that group. We have dumped our human garbage of hate, fear and doubt into our spiritual sea for so long, we now have created a threat to our spiritual life. Some people may call this spiritual organism of garbage *evil* or *the devil*. Whatever name you place on it, the first step away from our earthly garbage dump is meditation. Continued meditation takes you quickly back to the sweet light of God.

Amusement is helpful in meditation as it lets you move above the heavier emotions of the body. So when you get discouraged by the cleansing project you have created, remember the garbage dump and realize that you can clear it if you simply persist and allow yourself some amusement about your creations. It is easier to clean up a mess when you are amused.

A dear friend of mine has a wonderful level of amusement. She is often laughing and smiling and brings joy to everyone around her. Recently she experienced a tragedy in her life. She fell into despair and lost contact with her amusement for two months. Her friends encouraged her, and she continued to meditate and stay spiritually focused to the best of her ability. One day she came to see me, she laughed and said, "I am taking myself much too seriously." I knew then that she would be her happy self again soon. Her meditation and amusement brought her through her dark valley and back into her spiritual light. Anyone can learn to meditate, the way my friend meditates, to shine light into his or her life.

Since most people find it difficult to sit still and focus enough to reach a state of quiet without assistance, there are techniques to help you to attain this space. The meditation techniques that follow can help you experience yourself, as spirit, and your communication with God. Like anything else in this reality, you have to use meditation for it to work for you. You cannot just read about it or think about it and still have it affect you because meditating is a spiritual process, not an intellectual process. You must sit down and consciously perform the techniques to experience any results. Remember, it took Jesus many years of using such meditation techniques to prepare for his public ministry, so please be patient and allow time for your meditations to affect your reality.

Be aware that you may begin to uncover aspects of yourself you do not like, and that this is part of the process. Since all things are permissible in this reality, you may have created many things you no longer want. Simply release what you do not want and strengthen what you like. Let go of self-judgement for the aspects of yourself you do not like. Emphasize the creations that are beneficial, and you will reach your goal of spiritual awareness. Be careful not to allow your judgement or expectations to stop you in your awakening. Accept yourself as you are, and you will blossom like a flower.

If you get discouraged when your prayers are not immediately answered or your meditations are not instantly bringing you the expected results, remember patience. Also remember that you are unlearning old ways of operating while learning an entirely new system of functioning in this reality. You are relearning the principles of spiritual communication and your oneness with God.

When you are beginning to meditate, it is important to realize that everything is energy. Electricity is a familiar form of energy, normally invisible to us, but visible when it passes through a light bulb. The chair on which you sit is composed of a denser form of energy. It is solid and has mass. Our bodies are made of energy that is less dense than the chair, yet more dense than the electricity. Words and thoughts are also energy. You, as spirit, are energy as well. You are a very high vibration of energy. You are a much higher vibration of energy than any of the physical reality, including your body.

Through meditation, you can begin to manipulate and use your spiritual energy consciously to create your reality. You can unlearn the concepts that say you are helpless and begin to see your power to create through your physical body. You can become aware of the differences between spirit and body and use them to enhance your reality. You can allow yourself to be the immortal, all-knowing, loving spirit and allow the body to be its mortal, limited self. You, the spirit, are not bound by time and space, while the body is. The body uses effort to achieve its goals, has mass and density, is competitive and communicates to you and to others with emotions.

You, the bright spark of light which is spirit, are not limited by these aspects of the body. You have chosen to take a body to learn through by using these physical phenomena. You learn by creating through the body. Meditation helps you be more consciously aware of yourself, as spirit, and of the body as your creative expression. Every experience you create is an opportunity to learn a spiritual lesson.

When you meditate, you realize that you need to raise the vibration of your body by cleansing debilitating energies from it. Spirit and body are meant to be in harmony and to work together. By communicating with your body during meditation, you can eventually bring the body vibration up to where you can move freely into it. You will also be relearning how the body functions and how you can best use its energies for your spiritual purpose.

Through meditation, you can take conscious control of your reality and enhance your communication with all things. Since you are a part of God and God is all things, the enhancement of your spiritual communication through meditation can bring peace and joy into your life.

*"When you have broken
through the clouds
just once and have
experienced the beauty
of communication
and oneness through
meditating, the process
becomes so meaningful
that it is difficult to
eliminate from your life."*

MEDITATION TECHNIQUES

These meditation techniques are spiritual mysteries handed down through the ages. The techniques help you, as spirit, gain mastery over your physical body and energetic system. You can change your life by using these techniques faithfully on a regular basis. Grounding, centering in your head, creating and destroying a rose and running energy help you, the spirit, to regain seniority with your body and to re-establish your awareness of yourself and God. The techniques are spiritual tools for you to use to quiet and cleanse your energetic system so you, the spirit, can create and communicate through it. You can experience a lifetime of spiritual opening and awareness by using these meditation techniques. These techniques are not to be worshipped, but are to be used to worship God.

Anyone can learn these powerful yet simple techniques, but you do need to practice each one. You cannot read and intellectualize a technique and expect any results. You must experience the technique. This takes time for the body to do. If at first your body does not feel anything, keep using the technique; eventually, your body will experience the effect of the technique.

Learning to meditate without a teacher physically present to guide you through the exercises creates an opportunity for you to learn to guide yourself. You will find it helpful to have a pencil and paper available to write notes to yourself. This will assist in your self-teaching process. You can review the notes you make of your experiences to enhance your use of the techniques and to validate your progress. Use this journal to learn more about the techniques and about you, the spiritual being, and your body. As you write down your experiences, they become more real to you.

Choose a quiet place. Meditation is an inward focus, so a quiet place will help you achieve this turning within. Meditation is to help you return to the awareness that everyone and everything is of a spiritual nature. To do this, you must first learn to know yourself. Thus, a spiritual journey consists of turning within to yourself. You find all of your answers within you. Meditation helps you be still and listen so you can hear yourself and God.

SIT COMFORTABLY in a straight-backed chair with your feet flat on the floor and your hands separated and resting in your lap. Keeping your hands and feet apart allows your energy to flow freely.

HAVE your spine as straight as you can. A straight spine allows your energy to flow smoothly and comfortably.

ALLOW TIME for your body to become comfortable with this posture. It may take you several sessions to feel at ease sitting this way.

TAKE A FEW SLOW, DEEP BREATHS to relax your body. Your breathing enhances your meditation and assists your communication with God by relaxing your body. Remind yourself throughout the meditation to breathe deeply to relax your body, release energy and cleanse your system.

CLOSE YOUR EYES and turn your attention inward. When you close your eyes, you tune out the physically visual world and tune in to the spiritual world within you.

WHENEVER YOU PRACTICE a technique, sit back and relax with your eyes closed so you can tune in to you. This posture and the turning within will assist you to achieve a quiet meditation space.

"Grounding helps your body to feel safe and more comfortable. It gives the body a sense of security as it assists you to deal with survival issues about being here on Earth."

GROUNDING

Grounding is the first technique to use as you start your meditation. Grounding is the creation of an energy cord from your body to the center of the Earth. You, the being, create the cord from your first chakra and allow it to flow to the center of the Earth. You have spiritual energy centers throughout your system called chakras. These chakras contain spiritual information you need for your creative endeavors. You will use the first chakra as a point from which to ground. It is located near the base of your spine. Grounding from the first chakra is the foundation for all of the other techniques.

Each person experiences reality differently, so allow your own experience. You may feel safer and more solid or you may feel whatever discomfort you have stored in your body. Grounding makes you more aware of your body and your experience in this physical reality. Grounding is the way you, as spirit, connect with the physical world and take charge of your creativity on Earth.

BE AWARE of your first chakra which is the energy center near the base of your spine. This chakra contains your information about how to relate to this reality. Chakras are energy centers that contain information and energy for you to use and master as spirit.

VISUALIZE an energy flow from this chakra, near the base of your spine, to the center of the Earth. The energy will flow through all physical matter, the chair, the floor, the Earth, until it reaches the center of the planet. Allow the grounding cord to be securely attached at your first chakra and at the center of the Earth.

RELAX AND EXPERIENCE the spiritual connection you have created with Earth. Notice how your body reacts to being grounded. Take a few deep breaths to focus your attention on you and your body.

THE BODY may have a different experience than you do. You, the being, may feel joy while the body may feel discomfort. You may be experiencing the joy of spiritual awareness while the body may be feeling what you have stored in it. Or your body may feel relaxed, peaceful or safe.

ALLOW YOURSELF to be still and listen to you and your body so you can get to know yourself and your body as you ground. Each individual will have a unique experience.

FOR AN EXERCISE, let go of the grounding cord, allowing it to flow down into the Earth, and notice what it is like to be ungrounded. Do you feel less safe, less at peace?

RE-ESTABLISH YOUR GROUNDING by letting the cord flow from your first chakra to the center of the Earth. Strengthen the connections at the first chakra and the center of the Earth. Take a few deep breaths and relax with your grounding, allowing yourself to experience its effect on you and your body.

Everyone is spirit and, as spirit, we have created this physical reality to help us learn about ourselves and our creative abilities. The planet Earth is our spiritual schoolhouse: it gives us a place to learn our spiritual lessons. Grounding helps us be connected to and focused on this physical reality so we can focus on our personal creativity and learn our specific lessons. It helps us feel safe in this reality as it puts us in charge of it. Grounding acts as a foundation on which we can safely build our spiritual awakening through meditation.

You can be grounded at all times. When you are standing, lying down, sitting, walking or doing anything at all, you can be grounded. The more you practice grounding, the more you will be grounded. Use it in your daily life as well as in your meditation time. It will soon become a natural part of your life experience and enhance your relationship with this world.

As you sit quietly, experiencing being grounded, be aware of the benefits of grounding. Grounding helps your body to feel safe and more comfortable. It gives the body a sense of security as it assists you to deal with survival issues about being here on Earth. When grounded, you are more in touch with this reality and so can respond to whatever is happening more easily.

Grounding makes the body safe so that you, as spirit, can project more of your energy into your body. It acts like an electrical ground, allowing you, the energetic spirit, to flow safely into and through the less energetic body. Grounding allows you to be more in charge of your reality as you can create more fully through the body without effort when you are grounded. You bring more of your spiritual self into the body when you are grounded. Grounding helps you to be centered as well as connected to this reality. You are more aware of this reality and able to be stronger in it when you are grounded; thus, you are not a "pushover." Grounding creates strength for your creativity.

FOR FUN, ASK A FRIEND to gently push with his or her hand against your shoulder while you are grounded and then again while you are ungrounded. Take a moment to make the transition from being ungrounded to being grounded. Notice the difference in your solidity and stability when you are grounded. This simple exercise can help you acknowledge the effect grounding has on your body.

GROUNDING HAS ANOTHER BENEFIT; you can use it to release energy from your system. Be grounded and release energy down your grounding cord and allow it to be neutralized at the center of the Earth. Release tension, unwanted concepts, foreign energies or anything else down your grounding cord. You can use the grounding cord to release anything from your body or energy system that you do not want, whether it is your creation or something you accepted from someone else.

RE-ESTABLISH YOUR GROUNDING from the first chakra to the center of the Earth. Take a few deep breaths and release tension in your body down the grounding cord.

BE QUIET for a moment and repeat this release of energy down your grounding. You can release anything this way. You may want to try it, for instance, if you become extremely emotional. You can take a deep breath and release an emotion such as your anger so you can feel more in control of your body. You can release anything in this way.

USE YOUR JOURNAL to record what you release during your meditation times. What did you release from your body? You will learn about yourself as you review this cleansing process. Writing about your discoveries during meditation will help you see patterns in your creativity and will also help you make the spiritual cleansing real to your body.

VISUALIZE your grounding cord flowing from your first chakra to the center of the Earth. To practice your grounding, get up and walk around the room. As you walk, be conscious of your grounding. Sit down, unground by letting go of your grounding cord, and then walk around the room again noticing the difference. Sit in your chair again and re-ground.

RELEASE any emotion that surfaced for you as you experienced the difference between being grounded and ungrounded. Let the emotion flow down your grounding cord.

TUNE INTO any tension in your body. Breathe deeply and allow the tension to flow down your grounding cord and out of your body. Focus on releasing the tension down your grounding until you feel your body relax.

EXPERIMENT WITH RELEASING different energies from your body. Talk with your body as you do this to create harmony with your body.

Your grounding helps you to be in charge of your body and your experiences in your body. Grounding allows you to connect both spirit and body to this reality and to release anything you no longer want to keep within the body. Grounding gives you a foundation and an energy release.

Practice grounding every day, both in your quiet meditations and in your daily life, and it will become a part of your way of operating. You can use your grounding to release distractions that interfere with your meditations so you can be centered and quiet. You can use your grounding at any time and place to be more centered, secure and in charge of your life as well as to release any unwanted energy.

Use your grounding to enhance the communication between you, the spiritual being, and your body. Use your grounding to be in control of your experience here on Earth. Let your grounding create a safe space for you to meditate and communicate with God. Grounding can help you create a peaceful and joyous experience in this life.

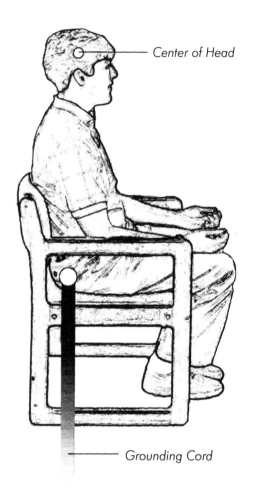

Center of Head

Grounding Cord

Figure 1: Grounding and Center of Head.

CENTER OF YOUR HEAD

T he next technique to learn is called the center of your head. You are spirit, and you appear in this reality as a bright spark of light. You have your physical body to create and communicate through in the physical plane. The center of your head is the place where you, as spirit, are meant to reside in the body. In the center of your head, you are able to remain neutral, without judging yourself or others. From this space, you have your spiritual perspective.

The center of your head is your neutral space where you can see what *is* instead of what you wish were true or what others wish you to see. The center of your head is where you can abide in the body and see your creations clearly. Being there is like being in the driver's seat of your car rather than in the back seat or the trunk. The center of your head is the place where you can be amused and in control of your reality. It is like the control tower for you, as spirit, in your body.

You, as spirit, can be anywhere. You can be outside of your body or in any part of your body or energy system.

The center of your head is where you are intended to sit in the body to best use and control your body and life experiences. Practice being in this neutral space where you have a clear spiritual view of life.

REMAIN SEATED with hands and feet separated and close your eyes. Ground yourself through the body from the first chakra to the center of the Earth.

FOCUS YOUR ATTENTION into the center of your head, behind and slightly above the level of your eyes. To help you experience this, place your index fingers, one just above your ear and one on your forehead between and slightly above your eyes. Imagine a line flowing into your head from the tip of each finger and notice where the lines would intersect. This is approximately the center of your head. Take away your fingers and allow yourself, as spirit, to be in that place.

FOCUS YOUR ATTENTION into the center of your head. As spirit, you go where you put your attention and, as spirit, you can be any place instantly.

BE IN THE CENTER of your head. Take a few deep breaths to allow your body to adjust to your presence. It may not be accustomed to you being there so strongly. Take time to experience your attention there and the effect this has on your body.

ALLOW YOURSELF to get a word or two to describe the experience to help make it more real for you and for your body. You may see yourself immediately as a bright light, or it may take you some time to see yourself there. Remember, you are a bright light and a part of God whether you are able to see yourself yet or not. Practice centering in your head, and eventually you will see the bright light of you.

NOTICE YOUR GROUNDING when you focus into the center of your head. Allow your grounding to increase to release any tension caused by you being in the center of your head.

YOU ARE SPIRIT and the body is your creation. You, the spirit, can get a reaction from the body upon entering it. This is when grounding is important to help the body deal with you because you have so much more energy than the body.

AS YOU EXPERIENCE being in the center of your head and grounded, relax and breathe deeply to quiet your thoughts. You can let the busyness of your thoughts flow away down your grounding cord to the center of the Earth. You can also release anyone else's thoughts you may have in your head down your grounding cord.

CENTER and experience this neutral space. Notice anything that is not yours and release it down your grounding.

RELEASE any foreign energy down your grounding cord, and own the center of your head for yourself by being there.

You are the only energy or spiritual being appropriate to be in the center of your head. This area is your control center in the body. Because spirit loves to communicate and share, you may find you have shared the center of your head with someone else. You may discover foreign or inappropriate energies in the center of your head because you believed they were appropriate. You are not meant to share this space with anyone since it is where you need to be to control your body and creativity.

The center of your head is the place from which you see and control what is happening in your reality. If someone else's energy is there, you will create your reality through their concepts and beliefs rather than through your own. You can communicate and create best if you have this space for yourself. Sharing the center of your head would be like sharing the driver's seat of your car, very confusing and possibly dangerous. You need to keep this space clear during meditation as it is part of the system with which you communicate with God.

It is often difficult for us to learn to be spiritually separate within our individual bodies since we are spiritually connected. We long to merge when we are in our bodies in the same manner that we can when we are not in a body. We must learn to be separate and centered in our individual body to learn our unique life lessons. If we merge with any other being, we will be learning his or her lessons and we will have to return in another body to learn our own lessons in another life. The center of the head is the neutral, non-judgmental space in which we learn with the greatest control and least confusion.

Many people believe that the heart chakra is the place to abide within the body, but this is not true. If you center in the fourth chakra, you will be overwhelmed with its vibration, the body's desires and emotions and other people's energies and emotions. You will not be able to stay in control of your creativity if you center in the fourth chakra. When you focus in the center of your head, you can have the vibration of oneness from the heart chakra without being overwhelmed or confused by this chakra or the body. If you center in the heart chakra, you will not learn your unique lessons because you will not be neutral and you will be experiencing other people's energies very strongly. Your spiritual, unique view of life is seen from the center of your head.

Being in the center of your head puts you in neutral with yourself and others. It is a safe place for you, as spirit, to create in this reality. It is the space where you can be on the Earth and yet not of it. Being in the center of your head, in neutral, allows you to have your amusement about your creations. When you have this neutral view of life, you maintain your spiritual perspective and do not allow yourself to be drawn into the darkness of the ego. You begin to see clearly what *is* rather than what you or others wish to have you see. In other words, you see beyond the facades of this world and you see the spiritual reality.

TO HELP YOU be more certain about being centered, allow yourself to experience other spaces as spirit. Move your attention above your head and experience the difference. Get a word for being above your head as opposed to being in the center of your head. Move your awareness back to the center of your head.

MOVE YOUR ATTENTION to other places, and then back to the center of your head after every journey. First move to your right index finger and back, then into your left big toe and back to the center of your head.

EACH TIME, allow time to be aware of how each place feels to you and how your body responds to you being there. Hopefully, the finger and big toe locations will help you experience your amusement as you learn these techniques.

BREATHE DEEPLY, be grounded and focus your attention into the center of your head. Relax there as long as you are comfortable. The more you practice this, the easier it is for you to operate from this space. Increase the time spent there a little each day.

As you have undoubtedly discovered by now, the center of your head is a more effective place from which to run your reality than any other. The view is neutral and not judgemental. The body feels safe with you in charge in the center of your head. The spiritual space located there contains or allows easy access to all the information you need. The center of your head is where you can focus your energy intensely into this reality like the sunlight through a magnifying glass, or light reflecting through a crystal.

When you meditate, the center of your head is the place from which you can use your body as a communication system to communicate with God. As you practice meditation, the spiritual system in your head will open and develop. When you put your spiritual attention into the center of your head, you trigger this development. Meditate daily and the center of your head will become a neutral creative space for you.

"If you communicate with the body as you train it to be used for meditation, you create harmony with it. By communicating with the body, you establish affinity and openness with it."

CORNER OF THE ROOM

W e are spirit. We can be any place instantly. The body takes time and space to travel, but spirit is not bound by time and space. We can project ourselves by simply putting our attention where we want to go. We can experience being outside of the body by simply focusing our attention out of our body.

Focusing your attention into the center of your head allows you to experience and be in charge of your physical reality and creations. Being in the corner of the room allows you to experience yourself, as spirit, separate from the body. Going to the corner of the room during meditation is a safe way to journey outside of your body. Leaving your body consciously can help you experience and validate yourself as spirit and your spiritual characteristics.

Since you are not in as much control of your body when you are outside of it, it is recommended you go to the corner only when you are meditating in a safe place.

BE SEATED, with hands and feet separated, and close your eyes. Ground yourself through the body from the first chakra to the center of the Earth. Focus your attention into the center of your head.

NOW YOU ARE READY to experience leaving your body consciously and safely. First, open your eyes and turn in your chair until you can see the back of the room. Pick out an upper back corner of the room; this will be your destination. Now the body knows where you will be. Face forward again in your chair, close your eyes, ground, center and take a deep breath.

FLOAT up above your head, and then up to the corner of the room. Experience yourself, as spirit, outside of your body in the corner of the room. Stay there a moment. Slowly float back down to your body, stop above your head, and then gently move back down into the center of your head.

BE IN THE CENTER of your head and experience being surrounded by your body. Take a deep breath and relax your body. Use your grounding to release any tension your body experienced from having you leave it.

You have consciously created an out-of-body experience. When you do this consciously, while remaining grounded, you do it safely. If you are not conscious of leaving the body and are ungrounded, you may frighten your body. Be aware of how your body feels about you leaving it and going to the corner. Notice how your body feels about you being back in the center of your head. You are learning to work with the body, instead of forcing it to do what you wish.

If you communicate with the body as you train it to be used for meditation, you create harmony with it. By communicating with the body, you establish affinity and openness with it. You can use your meditations to cleanse the body and learn to communicate with it. As you clear the body of the pain of being forced to comply with your demands and instead start working harmoniously with it, you create the communication system you seek. When the body is clear, your communication with God is clear.

Going to the corner of the room helps you recognize yourself, as spirit, separate from your body. You are not your body; you are spirit. As spirit you do not use effort. The body does use effort. You can experience no-effort in the corner of the room.

SIT with your spine straight, with hands and feet separated and close your eyes. Ground yourself through the body from the first chakra to the center of the Earth. Focus your attention into the center of your head.

FLOAT UP above your head, and then up to the corner of the room again; experience the no-effort flow of you, as spirit. Be in the corner of the room and experience yourself as spirit, without effort.

RETURN to the center of your head and experience being surrounded by the effort energy of your body. You, as spirit, can be amused by effort when you know you are not your body. You can also allow the body its own way of functioning when you realize you are spirit and not limited by the body.

TRY THIS EXERCISE to help you experience the effect of being in and out of the body: write a column of numbers on a sheet of paper. Ground and go from the center of your head to the corner of the room. Add the numbers while grounded and in the corner of the room. Then come gently back to the top of your head and back into the center of your head.

COUNT THE NUMBERS again after you have grounded and centered in your head. Notice the difference in your ability to do the exercise in and out of your body. Release anything you wish to let go of down your grounding. This exercise can help you realize how being out of your body affects your ability to function in the physical world.

REPEAT THE TECHNIQUE of going to the corner of the room and returning to the center of your head until you are comfortable with it. Simply moving from the center of your head to the corner of the room and back can help you become more aware of yourself, as spirit. Think of words that describe both experiences to help you identify with both realities.

During your meditations, you can be in the center of your head to help you solve problems related to your body. To solve spiritual problems, you can go to the corner of the room and leave the limits of the body behind. Examples of body problems are: finding a place to live or a new job. Some examples of spiritual problems are: learning how to change a behavior pattern or how to enhance your communication, or developing seniority with your body.

As we learn that we are spirit and have a body to use to communicate in this reality, we also need to learn how to function both in and out of the body. We can awaken to our spiritual selves and learn to focus into the body to learn our physical lessons and to move out of the body for our spiritual needs. Going to the corner of the room can provide us with the space we need from our physical creations to validate our spiritual nature.

Going to the corner of the room is an exercise to be used during your quiet meditations to help you regain your spiritual perspective. It would be confusing to do this exercise in work or play because you do not have the body control necessary when you are out of your body to remain safe during physical activities. Whenever you meditate, allow time to go to the corner of the room to experience yourself, as spirit, without being surrounded by the limits of the physical body.

"We believe we can think about things to learn them, but we have to practice and experience spiritual techniques to learn them... When we allow ourselves to expand into our spiritual awareness, we go beyond all physical limits, including the intellect."

SPIRITUAL EXPERIENCE

Allow your meditations to be a spiritual experience. If you have difficulty experiencing one of these techniques, just relax with it for awhile. If you get caught in trying to figure out how to experience a technique, move on to the next technique and return to that one later. These are spiritual techniques, and you need to operate as spirit to experience the techniques and their effect on you and your body. This requires using the techniques as spirit, without effort.

Each time you repeat the technique, you will grow more in confidence and experience more. It may take a few times using some particular technique for you to physically sense it. Experience is the only way to learn this information since it is spiritual and not intellectual. Repetition of the techniques is essential to train the body to allow you, as spirit, to be senior with the body. Thus, daily meditation will bring the best results in your experience of yourself, as spirit, and the response of your body to you.

We have all become focused on the intellectual process of learning which is an aspect of the physical world. We believe we can think about things to learn them, but we have to practice and experience spiritual techniques to learn them. These spiritual techniques require that we move into a higher level of awareness and operate as spirit. This demands a leap of faith in the beginning as it often takes time for the body to adjust to the new way of being used. The body is comfortable with its intellectual process, but the intellect is limited in its scope, like a computer. When we allow ourselves to expand into our spiritual awareness, we go beyond all physical limits, including the intellect.

As you continue to use the techniques, you will relearn how to operate as spirit with all that is available in your body. The intellect will become a part of this, but no longer an upper limit. Through continued meditation, you can become aware of reality beyond the physical realm.

Time also creates confusion as you begin to awaken spiritually. Your body operates in time and you, as spirit, do not. You need to allow time for your body to adjust to your new way of working with it while you, as spirit, will adjust instantly. Be patient with your body and it will respond to you, as spirit, allowing your spiritual experience within it.

Operate as spirit and your creativity is no longer limited by your body. As you use the techniques to meditate, allow the awakening of your spiritual experience and the rejuvenating of your body.

*"Each person has
the Divine spark
within, waiting
to ignite and be
a light. When
the light shines,
the darkness
melts away."*

CREATING AND DESTROYING

Our spiritual ability to create and destroy is another ingredient in meditation. We need to be able to destroy to clear away old concepts and make room for new ones. We must create to make the new in our lives. We need to be able to both create and destroy to heal and change. If we create without destroying, we become a slave to our creations; and we cannot destroy without creating to fill the new space. We need both sides of this dichotomy to balance our creativity.

There are many physical examples of the need to have both ends of this dichotomy. The seasons show us the healing powers of creation and destruction as we watch things change and see each phase play its part in the Earth's process. As with the seasons, chemical reactions and all things, when one thing is destroyed, another is created. When wood is destroyed by burning, fire, warmth and ashes are created.

We can see the creative-destructive cycles of Earth all around us. In addition to the seasons and chemical changes, there are the life cycles of all living things to show us Earth's creative cycles. All living things experience birth, growth and death. Creation is one of God's gifts to us in this reality, and meditation can assist us to use this gift consciously and beneficially.

In this exercise, we use the image of a rose as it represents the opening of the individual soul to God. As a rose opens to the sun, the soul opens to God. It is also a symbol of beauty, neutrality and simplicity. We will use the rose symbol to practice conscious spiritual creativity. By creating and destroying the symbol of a rose, we activate and cleanse our spiritual system.

SIT BACK in your chair, ground from your first chakra to the center of the Earth, close your eyes and be in the center of your head. Take a few deep breaths to help you center and ground.

CREATE A MENTAL IMAGE picture of a rose about six inches out in front of your forehead. Admire your creation. Now, destroy the rose. You can explode the rose like a firecracker, let it melt away or simply let it disappear. When you do this, you free the energy to be reused. Notice how you feel as you do this.

CREATE ANOTHER ROSE and destroy it. Use a different way to let it go. Be aware that you are clearing your spiritual and physical spaces as you do this. This exercise assists you to create change in your reality. You can release energy down your grounding that interferes with your ability to either create or destroy the rose.

CREATE another rose and admire your creation. Reach out with your hand and feel the rose. All creations occupy space, and you can feel the rose once you sensitize yourself. Explode the rose and reach out and feel its absence.

CREATE AND EXPLODE ROSES for a moment. Simply create a rose, then explode it, and repeat this at your own rate. Be grounded and centered as you do this.

ALLOW TIME to practice this exercise. Practice this spiritual ability and release any expectations you may have about it. Find a few words to describe this experience to yourself.

Creating and destroying roses helps you release concepts that no longer work for you. This makes it easier for you to get in touch with your unique information. As you become clearer, you are able to create what is correct for you in the present. For example, you may be afraid of crossing the street since you are still operating from the information given to you by an adult when you were a child. You can destroy this person's information now, and create your own awareness of how to cross the street. Another example is seeing someone through another person's opinion. You can destroy that other person's concepts and have your own opinion. These simple examples can be expanded to any aspect of your life.

FOCUS ON YOUR GROUNDING and be in the center of your head. Create a rose in front of you. Get in touch with a belief of yours that keeps you from being creative. Let the belief float into the rose and then destroy the rose. You have just consciously created your reality. You changed your spiritual reality by clearing something you no longer want. You changed your view of this reality by letting go of a limit to your creativity.

CREATE ANOTHER ROSE. Be aware of a belief that stops you from creating the image of a rose. Release the belief into the rose and explode the rose. You cleared another limit to your creativity.

DO THE SAME for anything interfering with your ability to destroy in your reality. Create a rose, release into it any interference to your ability to destroy anything you do not want, and explode the rose.

YOU CONSCIOUSLY cleared another limit to your creativity. We need to destroy in order to create as these abilities are complementary. Like two halves of the same circle, neither is complete without the other.

CREATE another rose. Be aware of a belief that limits your ability to explode a rose and let it flow into the rose; then explode that rose.

Practice creating and exploding roses during your meditations. Each time you do this, you change your energy. You are consciously changing your reality by clearing your space. You can direct your meditations by consciously creating a rose to represent what you wish to clear and exploding the rose.

You can create and destroy roses to help you ground, center in your head and perform the other techniques. This technique is an example of your spiritual creativity. By doing this, you make a statement about yourself as a creative, aware spirit.

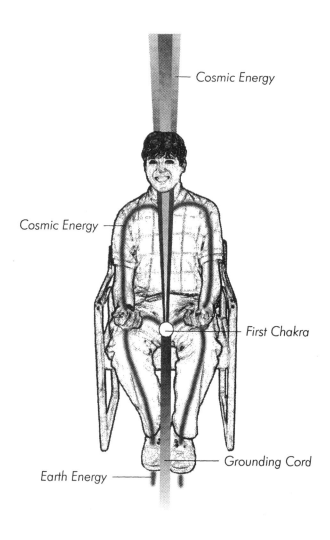

Cosmic Energy

Cosmic Energy

First Chakra

Grounding Cord

Earth Energy

Figure 2: Running Energy.

RUNNING ENERGY

Another technique to assist you in quieting the mind-body system and taking charge as spirit is consciously running your energy. We all run energy since all living things have energy and energy is in motion. This technique is a way of moving your energies consciously, in a particular pattern, to enhance your relationship with both the physical reality and the spiritual realm.

We use earth and cosmic energies to balance body and spirit. We are spirit and we have a body through which to create and communicate. We need to understand and learn to use the body as well as to remember how to operate as spirit in a body. Running earth and cosmic energies helps us with this learning process. These energies also help us cleanse both the physical and spiritual systems for an enhanced spiritual awareness. Running energy is an important technique for meditation.

We begin with earth energy, the energy of the planet. Earth energy enhances your grounding and assists you to be more aware of this reality and how to operate in it. It also helps your body feel real and safe. Earth energy helps you be in touch with how the physical world works. Part of your lesson in any lifetime is how to operate a body and how to function in time and space. Grounding and earth energy help you focus on the body as your creative vessel or door into this reality. When you are focused, you can accomplish your mission here.

Think of life as a game. If you know how the game works, what the rules are and concentrate on the game, then you play it well. If you are not focused, do not know or follow the rules and do not use your body correctly, the game will not work for you. Life can be compared to playing soccer. If you prepare your body, practice and focus on the game, you play well and with enthusiasm. If your body is not prepared and you do not focus on the play, you will not have fun or play well. Earth energy helps you stay in touch with the game of life here on Earth.

Your body and the planet are yours through which to create. You have to own this reality and attach to it to operate effectively through it. You need to learn how to own and use your body and how to project through it. It is necessary to heal the body and be in harmony with your earthly creations to accomplish your spiritual purpose. Use your earth energy and grounding to assist you to be in touch with your body and your other earthly creations.

SIT UPRIGHT in a chair, back straight, feet on the floor and hands separated. Sitting straight will enhance the flow of energy. Close your eyes, ground, center and turn within.

BE AWARE of your feet on the floor. There are chakras, or spiritual energy centers, in the arches of your feet. The chakras can be opened and closed like the lens of a camera. Open your feet chakras. Allow earth energy to flow up through these energy centers and to flow through channels that run up through your legs to the first chakra near the base of your spine.

AT THE FIRST CHAKRA, allow the energy to flow down your grounding cord. Be centered and grounded and experience this movement of energy through your feet chakras, up your leg channels and down your grounding cord. Be aware of how earth energy affects your grounding.

ALLOW TIME to experience the earth energy flowing. Notice how your body reacts to it. From the center of your head, notice how you experience this energy. Take a few deep breaths to assist the energy to flow more freely.

RELAX and allow the earth energy to move up your legs and down your grounding. You may also find it helpful to stand up and move around the room as you run this earth energy to experience that you can use it at all times. Then be seated again and experience the earth energy from this more focused perspective.

EARTH ENERGY helps you relate to the Earth. Take a deep breath and experience the flow of this energy through the channels in your legs and down the grounding.

IF YOU FEEL *spacey* or out of touch with the physical world, you can ground and run earth energy to bring yourself back to Earth and this reality. This energy of the Earth assists you to relate more clearly to your physical reality and gives you a sense of oneness with your world.

TAKE A FEW DEEP BREATHS and experience the flow of earth energy up the channels in your legs and down your grounding cord. Relax with this and allow your body to enjoy this flow of energy. Let the energy be like warm water flowing and melt away any tension in your legs.

Next, we add cosmic energy which is the unlimited energy of the Cosmos. Cosmic energy is experienced as vibrations and seen in this reality as colors. We have an infinite variety of cosmic vibrations to use. We can use any color we choose according to our needs. For now, we will use a bright gold energy since gold is a neutral vibration. When we consciously bring cosmic energy into our system, we take charge of our spiritual relationship with this reality. The cosmic energy helps us to raise the body's vibration so we can bring more of our spiritual energy into the body. When we focus our attention into the body, we are better able to communicate through it and fulfill our earthly purpose.

CREATE A BALL OF GOLD cosmic energy above your head. This configuration will help make cosmic energy more real to your body. Allow the energy to flow down to the top of your head. Let it flow into your body at the top of your head and flow along channels on each side of your spine, all the way down to the first chakra.

ALLOW THE EARTH ENERGY to blend with the cosmic energy at your first chakra. Then let the blend of energies flow up channels running through your body, until it fountains out the top of your head and flows like a fountain all around your body.

ALLOW MORE COSMIC ENERGY to flow than earth energy as the blend of energies moves up through the body past the heart area. The energy system needs the cosmic energy in the upper areas of the system as it relates more to spirit. The lower centers of the body relate more to physical creativity. Allow the excess earth energy to flow down the grounding cord to enhance the grounding.

LET SOME OF THE ENERGY branch off at the cleft of your throat and move down channels in your shoulders and arms and out the chakras, or energy centers, in the palms of your hands. The energies in your arms and hands are your creative and healing energies. You use these energies to create on the physical plane.

FOCUS in the center of your head, be grounded and experience this flow of energies. The earth energy moves up the legs and down the grounding. The cosmic energy flows down the back channels along each side of the spine. It mixes with some earth energy in the first chakra near the base of your spine, then moves up through channels in the body, to fountain out the top of the head and flow all around you.

ALSO ALLOW ENERGY to branch off at the throat and flow out the arms. Allow the energies to melt away any interference to the flow of energies in the channels like warm water melting ice.

Allow time to run your energy. It is a technique that helps you clear your body and spiritualize it for your use. Allow the process to be easy and effortless. If you are experiencing effort, use your grounding to release tension. You can also create and destroy roses to let go of anything that is causing you to be in effort. Simply create and explode a rose several times to release energy. You can visualize the earth and cosmic energies being like clear water, flowing and cleansing. Like a flowing stream cleanses and purifies as it moves, so your earth and cosmic energies act as a cleansing flow through your system.

Because these are spiritual techniques, you have to learn to use them as spirit. This requires letting go of intellectualizing them and allowing yourself to simply practice your techniques. Everything is energy. You can manipulate energy to create what you want. Let go of the fixation on the body's perspective and tune into the spiritual view that everything is energy and is in motion. You need to re-establish your spiritual consciousness in the body, and practicing these techniques helps you do this.

YOU CAN RELEASE any effort or other body energies down your grounding. Do it now by taking a deep breath and sending any tension down your grounding cord. Also, create and explode roses to release body tension and to allow you, as spirit, to be in charge.

BE IN THE CENTER of your head and experience how it feels to have your energies flowing. Have you felt this before or does it feel new? Get to know yourself spiritually and physically so you can create your reality consciously.

BE STILL and enjoy the flow of earth and cosmic energies through your system. Let the earth energy, flowing through the chakras in your feet and up the channels in your legs, flow to your first chakra and down your grounding cord.

BRING THE GOLD cosmic energy down through the channels in the top of your head, and through the channels along each side of your spine, to your first chakra near the base of your spine.

MIX THE EARTH AND COSMIC energies at the first chakra, and let the blend flow up through the channels running through your body. Feel it branch off at the cleft of your throat, and flow through the channels in your arms and out your hands. Feel it flow out the top of your head and all around you.

ALLOW TIME to be quiet and run your energies. Let your body feel the energy flow through it. Release tension, foreign and inappropriate energies by running your earth and cosmic energies.

BE STILL and enjoy the flow of earth and cosmic energies without thought or consideration for anything. Simply be.

By bringing the earth and cosmic energies into and through your system, you balance spirit and body. You experience your earthly reality while maintaining awareness of your spiritual nature. The conscious manipulation of these energies assists you to experience yourself, as spirit, manifesting in a physical body.

By running our energies, we raise the vibration of our body. This allows us to come more into the body and use it more effectively for our spiritual purposes. Using the technique of running energy to cleanse the system and raise the vibration assists our meditations. Since the purpose of meditation is to communicate with God and our higher selves, the system must be cleansed for this purpose.

Create a quiet time for yourself to run your energy every day. Each time you will create more clarity and thus more open communication. Allow yourself time to be in the center of your head, ground, and experience the flow of earth and cosmic energies through your system. These techniques help you develop your system for communication with God.

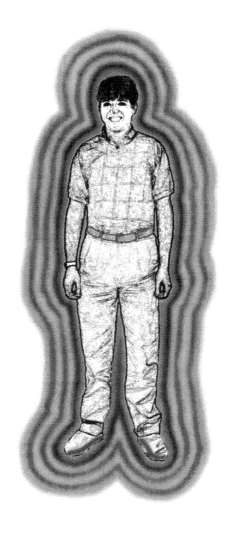

Figure 1: The Aura.

THE AURA

Each living thing has an energy field. This energy field is your aura. Your aura indicates your psychic or spiritual space, and is your universe in which you are meant to create. It is the window through which you view the world and through which the world sees you. Your aura changes as you change your energy. The aura is seen in this reality as colors and ideally goes all around your body.

Your aura emanates from your seven major chakras or spiritual energy centers. The energy centers are located along your spine from the base of your spine to the top of your head. Typically, there are seven layers of the aura emanating from these seven chakras. Some souls have more and others have fewer layers of their aura depending on their level of development. Your aura is the manifestation of your energy seen as colors.

The colors of the aura are not as significant as the clarity and motion of energy. Running earth and cosmic energies helps cleanse and clear your aura and create motion through it. You increase your vibration as you run your energies and meditate. You cleanse the energy, and thus the colors in your aura, which makes your aura clearer and brighter. The flow of energies also increases the motion of your aura and creates the higher vibration.

FOCUS YOUR AWARENESS into the center of your head. Establish your grounding. Allow your energies to run. Bring earth energy up through your feet and leg channels and down your grounding. Bring cosmic energy through the top of your head and down the channels on either side of your spine.

MIX THE EARTH AND COSMIC energies at your first chakra and bring them up the front channels and out of the top of your head. Let the energies branch off at the cleft of your throat and flow down your arms and out your hands.

AS YOUR ENERGY flows out the top of your head, let it flow like a fountain all around you. Let the flow of energy clear and cleanse your aura as it manifests all around your body.

FROM THE CENTER of your head, be aware of your aura, your energy field. Allow it to be over your head, around your torso and under your feet. Let it flow behind you and in front of you, all around you like an egg shell around an egg. Make sure it comes down under your feet so you are engulfed in your own aura.

FROM THE CENTER of your head, experience the flow of energy through your aura. The aura is in motion and so is the energy flowing through it. Be still in the center of your head and enjoy the flow of energy.

TO ALLOW YOURSELF experience and awareness of your aura, expand your aura to encompass the room you are in now. Be aware of how this feels. It may be familiar to you if you are in the habit of doing this to be in touch with or in control of your environment. If you expand your aura to the size of the room and there are other people in the room, you will be experiencing their realities as well as your own. You may feel confused or disoriented or you may feel normal if this is your usual way of relating to the world.

YOUR AURA is like a bubble of energy surrounding you. Because it is your unique energy, you need to allow it to be close enough around you so that you do not experience other people's realities by engulfing them in your aura.

CONTRACT YOUR AURA until it is close around your body. Experience having it very close. This may also feel uncomfortable as you are not allowing much personal space. This may remind you of how you feel in an elevator or other close quarters. Notice the feeling so you can be aware of how you are relating to your aura and can change it when you wish.

FOCUS ON BEING GROUNDED and centered in your head. Take a few deep breaths and relax your aura to a comfortable distance from your body. You may find that from six to eight inches around your body is comfortable in most circumstances.

YOU CAN ADJUST your aura at any time. You can expand it or contract it depending on your circumstances. For example, many people contract their individual aura in a threatening situation but often expand their aura to experience others during a concert or other shared musical performance.

BE IN THE CENTER of your head, be grounded and experience your aura flowing around you. Visualize being surrounded by color in motion. Take a deep breath and release any excess energy down your grounding.

We manifest our energy through our space as vibrations which can be seen in our aura as colors. Everything that has consciousness of life manifests the condition of its being in the form of energy waves. This energy field is the aura. This space is for our spiritual creativity in this physical reality.

Your aura and everything inside it is your spiritual universe in this reality. To fully experience yourself, you need to have your aura around your body only. When you meditate, pull your aura around you and experience yourself. Your meditations are a time for you to experience your unique vibration and creativity.

*"You create your
experience in the
physical world by
desiring something
and believing in it.
If you desire to
communicate with God
and believe you can,
then you will."*

GUIDED MEDITATION

The techniques of grounding, focusing in the center of your head, going to the corner of the room, creating and destroying roses, running earth and cosmic energies and controlling your aura all assist you with increasing your spiritual awareness. As you practice the techniques, you will experience more of yourself, as spirit. You will be taking seniority over your body and your creations in this physical reality. Have patience and your meditations will bring you new insights into yourself and your creations. Your meditations will eventually bring you to your communication with God.

Your meditations are a time for you to communicate with yourself, your body and your God. Practice the techniques and allow them to help you to reach a state of peace where you can experience this level of spiritual communication. As in all things, you will need to practice the techniques for them to work for you. To begin with, a half hour a day is beneficial. You can even divide this into two segments if you need to, until you can meditate comfortably for the full thirty minutes. As you develop your clarity, you may learn to enjoy two thirty-minute segments a day. Eventually, you can learn to enjoy an hour or more of meditation each day. This reality is meant to be enjoyed, so allow your meditations to be a joyous experience.

GROUND, take a deep breath and relax with your grounding. Allow the grounding cord to flow from your first chakra, near the base of your spine, to the center of the Earth. Attach the cord firmly at both the first chakra and the center of the Earth. Relax and use your grounding to release any tension in your body.

BE IN THE CENTER of your head. Use your index fingers to help you locate the physical place in the center of your head. Breathe deeply and allow time to experience being behind your eyes, in the center of your head. Focus your attention there and experience being surrounded by your body. Be focused in this neutral place. See yourself as a bright light in the center of your head.

GO TO THE CORNER of the room. Look at an upper back corner of the room. Let you, the spiritual being, float above your head and move freely to the corner of the room. Experience being out of your body. Be aware of yourself as separate from your body. Be aware that you are not your body. Allow your body to be as it is.

COME BACK to the center of your head. Flow smoothly and gently back down to the top of your head and then into the center of your head. Be aware of being surrounded by your body again.

CREATE A ROSE. Admire your creation. Reach out with your hand and feel where the rose occupies space in front of your forehead. Put your hand down.

EXPLODE THE ROSE. Be aware of your ability to create and destroy in order to create your reality. Reach out and feel the empty space and notice the difference.

CREATE AND DESTROY ROSES. Focus in the center of your head, be grounded and create and destroy roses for a few minutes to clear your space. Practice melting the roses, exploding them or just letting them disappear until you find your favorite way to let them go.

RUN YOUR EARTH ENERGY. Open your feet chakras and let the earth energy flow up through these chakras in the arches of your feet. Let the energy flow through the leg channels up your legs to your first chakra, and then down your grounding cord.

RUN YOUR COSMIC ENERGY. Create a ball of bright gold energy above your head, allow it to flow into the top of your head, and down channels along each side of your spine. Let the energy flow to the first chakra, near the base of your spine.

MIX THE COSMIC energy with some earth energy, and let the combination flow up through the channels running through your body. Let the energy fountain out the top of your head and flow all around you. Let some of the energy branch off at the cleft of your throat and flow down the channels in your arms and out the palms of your hands.

RUN YOUR ENERGY. Be grounded and quiet in the center of your head. Allow the earth and cosmic energies to flow through your system cleansing it. For a few minutes, focus on the flow of energies, being in the center of your head, grounding and creating and destroying roses.

BE AWARE OF YOUR AURA. From the center of your head make sure it is all the way around your body, under your feet, over your head, in back and in front of you. Let your energy fountain out of the top of your head and flow all around you and your body. Again sit quietly and experience the energies flowing through you and through your aura.

FOCUS IN THE CENTER OF YOUR HEAD. Enhance your grounding. Experience the flow of your energies. Be aware of your desire to communicate with God.

BE STILL AND LISTEN. Allow your communication with God.

You create your experience in the physical world by desiring something and believing in it. If you desire to communicate with God and believe you can, then you will. The meditation techniques help you cleanse and heal your system so you have a clear communication, unencumbered by inappropriate or foreign energies. Meditate regularly and you will awaken to your spiritual nature and your communication with God.

"As you take your spiritual awareness into your life, you not only benefit yourself, you also benefit all those around you. You will learn how to be more tolerant, more neutral and soon will experience the vibration we are here to manifest: love."

ASK AND YOU SHALL RECEIVE

You must ask in order to receive. Information will flow to you from the spiritual realm when you open yourself to it. You then need to listen in order to hear the information. The techniques will help you create a safe, quiet space for this spiritual communion.

The guidance you receive can relate to any aspect of your life. It is helpful to ask about what you need to know and then listen quietly for an answer. In the beginning, you will need to return to the meditation techniques often to keep your system clear and to maintain your focus.

You may find the information you receive to be unclear to you at first. If you are confused or unfocused, use the techniques to return to a clear, spiritually focused space. You may need to cleanse someone else's information, strong emotion or some other interference to your clarity. You may need to meditate on the information to gain a spiritual perspective of this new level of spiritual insight. Often the information cannot be understood in physical terms.

Be aware that the information is of a spiritual nature, and you may need time to fully comprehend it. You will eventually learn how to translate the spiritual information into your physical reality. For example, the Old Testament contains a symbolic message about destroying our bestial nature and focusing on our spiritual selves. This was misinterpreted and resulted in the sacrificing of animals to God. Be aware of the spiritual interpretation, and you will understand the true meaning of your information.

You can benefit during your entire life by using a spiritual perspective in every aspect of your reality. Meditation can help you receive spiritual information to guide you on your path for this life. You can ask about the meaning of your work, the solution to a problem or the way to improve a relationship. Any time you become unclear in the communication, or are having difficulty being quiet or hearing an answer, return to the techniques to clear your space. When you have prepared your system with the techniques, simply being quiet and receiving what is given can be the greatest healing of all.

As you take your spiritual awareness into your life, you not only benefit yourself, you also benefit all those around you. You will learn how to be more tolerant, more neutral and soon will experience the vibration we are here to manifest: love.

As we meditate, we raise our vibration, the vibration of our body, the vibration of all of our creations and even the vibration of the planet. As we solve our physical and spiritual problems and increase our vibration, we automatically assist others and the planet. When we fill ourselves with light, it shines out all around us.

SUGGESTED QUESTIONS

When you wish to consciously guide your meditations for a particular purpose or goal, you can ask specific questions. You may ask any question. You will not receive help if you wish to harm yourself or anyone or anything else. The answers may be clear to you or may take you some time to comprehend. If you have any difficulty, return to the meditation techniques and have faith that they will help you clear your system so you can have the communication you seek.

When you meditate and are quiet enough to listen, you may want to ask questions similar to these:

What is my spiritual path?

How can I best heal my body?

On what do I need to put my attention to follow my spiritual path?

How can I improve my relationship with _____? (This can include anything outside yourself such as your spouse, family, friends, job, etc.)

How can I best communicate with God?

What are my reasons for having a body this lifetime?

What is affecting my flow of energy?

How can I best serve God?

How can I best serve humankind?

What is my lesson for today?

Remember, you must be quiet and listen to receive the information. You may also need to meditate on the information to understand its meaning. It may take some time for you to interpret the information so it is comprehensible to your body.

As you meditate and increase your awareness, stay focused on the fact that everything and everyone is a part of God. God is in all things. When you use the techniques to clear the limits you have created and allowed within and around you, you begin to participate in life with greater spiritual awareness. You see that you can communicate directly with God Consciousness and with any of the great teachers such as Jesus Christ, Buddha, Mohammed or others. Each person has the Divine spark within, waiting to ignite and be a light. When the light shines, the darkness melts away.

We simply need to remember our Divine origin and release the limits of our physical world to return to our original state of grace which is in awareness of God. Meditation can be our bridge to this awareness. By turning within and becoming quiet, we can experience the awareness of light and re-establish both our joy in the Earth and our communion with God.

*"... everyone reflects each
other like mirrors.
Anything you do not
like in someone else
is something you
have not accepted
in yourself. What
you like in others
is an aspect
of you that you
need to validate."*

MEDITATING WITH OTHERS

Meditating with others can be a beneficial way to raise your vibration. You increase the vibration in your body when you meditate. When you meditate with others, everyone is raising his or her vibration, so you can reach an even higher vibration in a group. You go from one-candle power to two-, three- or more candle power depending on the number of people in the group.

The increased energy of the group helps the individual maintain his or her vibration at a high level. The bodies match and reinforce the higher vibration in each other. The higher vibration in the body allows the high energy spirit to more easily manifest in the body. The energies of spirit and body come closer so spirit can communicate better through the body.

Spirit is a very high vibration and the body is a lower vibration. We need to heal the body and raise its vibration so it is easier to use. Meditating with others can help you with this process as the interaction with others stimulates both spirit and body. Spirit and body both love communication, and group interaction provides communication on both levels.

You can reinforce your commitment to your meditation by meditating with a friend. You may encourage yourself to exercise by having a walking or aerobics *buddy*, and you can do the same with meditation. Just as in exercise, you each have to do your personal work, but you have the encouragement and stimulation of a friend doing the same thing. You can also talk about your meditations to help make them more meaningful for you. You do need to be aware that each person sees life through her personal concepts and experiences, so you must recognize the other person's perspective as her truth and not necessarily your truth. Each person has her personal view which needs to be respected, but not adopted.

To meditate with friends or family, everyone needs to use the same meditation techniques to create a balanced energy. Use the preceding techniques of grounding, centering and running energy together and enjoy the spiritual communication that comes from this. You can also listen to a meditation tape together to help you remain focused and on track.

I know several couples who meditate together. One couple was having difficulty in their relationship and their respective jobs. I suggested they meditate together to discover their problem and find solutions. They meditated together daily for two weeks and created a new level of communication and awareness. They continued their individual meditation daily and their couples' meditation three times a week. Through this renewed spiritual focus, they discovered the source of their relationship and work problems and started on a path of healing. The husband changed jobs and the wife learned to release judgement of her family; they both learned not to resist, as a result of their meditations together.

Another couple is happy to tell you that meditation saved their marriage. They were close to a divorce when they discovered this form of meditating and began practicing it daily. After meditating separately for several years, they added the joy of meditating together. Eventually, their daughter joined them to create a weekly family meditation time.

Meditating with a group can be difficult to choreograph, but can be worthwhile in many ways. You create a higher vibration, a support system, communication and the fun of being with like-minded people. Group meditation can also help you stay focused on your meditation for a longer period of time. A weekly meditation with a friend, group of friends or family members can be a fun addition to your meditation schedule. It can also create a healing connection in your family and friendship circles.

Creating a meditation group can be fun and supportive. It can also offer you a wealth of lessons from interacting with others on spiritual as well as physical levels. Any group interaction can teach you about yourself. Are you a leader or follower? Are you introverted or extroverted? Are you more physically or spiritually focused? The group can help you learn about yourself as everyone reflects each other like mirrors. Anything you do not like in someone else is something you have not accepted in yourself. What you like in others is an aspect of you that you need to validate. By seeing each member of the group as an aspect of yourself, you can learn a great deal.

The main danger of group meditation is one member playing power games with the others. If a member believes he knows more, is better or is superior, his ego is in charge and he is not operating as spirit. Someone may be capable enough to convince the remainder of the group he is worthy of adoration. The best way to identify if one member is *power tripping* in a group is if the group is no longer fun. Communication is the key to solving such problems. Talking about problems brings them into the light. Using the techniques to solve the problems helps everyone learn and grow.

A helpful technique to avoid having one person trying to control the group is to listen to meditation tapes together. The tape maintains a spiritual focus and helps defuse power struggles. It takes many years of self-healing for someone to earn the title of spiritual teacher, so be careful of someone in your group claiming to know more than others. Do not allow one unbalanced soul to interfere with the spiritual awakening of your group. Help the person balance and if he or she will not, ask that individual to leave your group. If the group, in fact, is controlled by this person, you can leave and start a new group with your increased awareness of the need for grounding and neutrality.

Most meditation groups, whether friends or family, will go through the usual stages for development of human groups. You need to let the group make mistakes and have successes, and to grow and mature. One idea the group can meditate on is releasing expectations of the group. This can help you have more fun. Meditating together is ideally fun. It is never perfect.

Meditation is an essential ingredient of spiritual awakening and growth. Meditating with others once a week can be a fun and rewarding addition to your daily meditations. Turn within and enjoy yourself and your traveling companions in this journey of life.

"By turning within and becoming quiet, we can experience the awareness of light and re-establish both our joy in the Earth and our communion with God."

SEEK AND YOU SHALL FIND

I hope this beginning meditation is helpful to you in seeking your spiritual information and communication. Allow the techniques and your desire to communicate with God to lead you through the difficult parts of the physical maze. Use the techniques any time you find yourself blocked or unclear, and they can help you find your path to God.

Have faith in yourself and your God, and everything else will follow. I have changed my own life with meditation, and I teach others to take charge of their creativity through meditation. Like the many people who called for help, let yourself find that help within you. Use this beginning meditation to lead you into yourself, where God abides and where all that you need is available. Every journey begins with one step. Take this small step of simple, beginning meditation and follow the path to your spiritual awareness.

Once you step onto the spiritual path, many things will open to you. When you master this simple meditation, other avenues will be open for you if you seek to continue your learning and growth. These powerful techniques are a foundation on which you can build your spiritual awareness. You can always use grounding, being in the center of your head and the other techniques to help you focus on yourself and your God, regardless of the spiritual path you choose.

God is always present; we only need to be present also. God is always aware of us; we only need to be aware of God. God loves everything and everyone; we need to remember how to love God.

God bless you.

INDEX

Mary Ellen Flora, spiritual teacher, healer and clairvoyant reader, has been sharing her remarkable insights on spirituality for many years. She is the leader of CDM, a spiritual community with seven locations. CDM is an international organization dedicated to spiritual freedom which she co-founded, over twenty years ago, with her husband, M. F. "Doc" Slusher.

Mary Ellen has taught meditation, healing, clairvoyance and other subjects, and has trained many others to teach, also. As a teacher, her focus has been on validating each individual's psychic abilities and helping people to recognize their spiritual nature.

She is also the author of numerous publications, including the *Key Series* and the *Energy Series* of inspirational and instructional books and audio-tapes.

Mary Ellen's dedication to spiritual freedom and personal growth, as well as her amusement and neutrality, have made her well-known as an inspirational and dynamic speaker. If you wish to contact Mary Ellen or have her speak to your group, please contact us at the following address or phone number:

CDM Publications
2402 Summit Avenue
Everett, WA 98201
Attn: Public Relations
1-800-360-6509

C DM is a spiritual community and an international organization dedicated to spiritual freedom. If you are interested in learning more about CDM, or want information about the following topics, please contact the **Church of Divine Man/CDM Psychic Institute**.

- Meditation
- Meditating with a group
- Clairvoyance
- Chakras
- Psychic Readings
- Healing
- Kundalini

**Church of Divine Man
CDM Psychic Institute**
2402 Summit Avenue · Everett, WA 98201
Phone: (425) 258-1449 · Fax: (425) 259-5109

Bellingham CDM
1311 "I" Street
Bellingham, WA 98225
(360) 671-4291

Seattle CDM
2007 NW 61st Street
Seattle, WA 98107
(206) 782-3617

Portland CDM
3314 SW First Avenue
Portland, OR 97201
(503) 228-0740

Tacoma CDM
4604 N. 38th
Tacoma, WA 98407
(253) 759-7460

Spokane CDM
c/o CDM
2402 Summit Avenue
Everett, WA 98201
(425) 258-1449

Vancouver CDM
2nd Floor
1564 W. 6th Avenue
Vancouver, BC V6J 1R2
(604) 730-8788

CDM Publications is a small press offering books and tapes of a spiritual nature. Our publications offer information to assist you in awakening to yourself, as spirit. Each publication offers easy-to-understand information on an aspect of spirituality and includes techniques to assist you in experiencing yourself, as spirit.

**CDM Publications
2402 Summit Avenue
Everett, WA 98201**

Phone: (425) 259-9322
Toll Free: 1-800-360-6509 · Fax: (425) 259-5109
E-mail: cdm@c-d-m.org · Website: www.c-d-m.org

**If you have questions or are
interested in learning more about
meditation, healing, clairvoyance
or other topics concerning spiritual
awareness, please contact us.**

CDM Publications
2402 Summit Avenue, Everett, WA 98201
Phone: (425) 259-9322 • Fax: (425) 259-5109 • Toll Free: 1-800-360-6509
E-mail: cdm@c-d-m.org • Website: www.c-d-m.org

		Quantity	Total
THE KEY SERIES BOOKS by Mary Ellen Flora			
Meditation: *Key to Spiritual Awakening*	$7.95 US / $11.00 Canadian	_____	_____
Healing: *Key to Spiritual Balance*	$7.95 US / $11.00 Canadian	_____	_____
Clairvoyance: *Key to Spiritual Perspective*	$10.00 US / $14.00 Canadian	_____	_____
Chakras: *Key to Spiritual Opening*	$10.00 US / $14.00 Canadian	_____	_____
THE KEY SERIES AUDIO CASSETTES by Mary Ellen Flora			
Meditation: *Key to Spiritual Awakening*	$9.95 US / $14.00 Canadian	_____	_____
Healing: *Key to Spiritual Balance*	$9.95 US / $14.00 Canadian	_____	_____
Clairvoyance: *Key to Spiritual Perspective*	$10.00 US / $14.00 Canadian	_____	_____
Chakras: *Key to Spiritual Opening*	$10.00 US / $14.00 Canadian	_____	_____
THE ENERGY SERIES BOOKS by Mary Ellen Flora			
Cosmic Energy: *The Creative Power*	$12.00 US / $16.00 Canadian	_____	_____
Earth Energy: *The Spiritual Frontier*	$12.00 US / $16.00 Canadian	_____	_____
Male & Female Energies: *The Balancing Act*	$15.00 US / $21.00 Canadian	_____	_____
Kundalini Energy: *The Flame of Life* (Hardbound Edition)	$40.00 US / $50.00 Canadian	_____	_____
OTHER BOOKS AVAILABLE			
I Believe: *Sermons* by M. F. "Doc" Slusher	$15.00 US / $21.00 Canadian	_____	_____
I Believe: *Sermons* (Hardbound Edition)	$30.00 US / $42.00 Canadian	_____	_____

SHIPPING & HANDLING:
$4.00 first item, $1.00 each additional item.
*Prices and availability subject
to change without notice.*
No cash or COD.

Sub-Total _____
Shipping & Handling _____
Tax (8.3% WA residents only) _____
TOTAL _____

☐ VISA ☐ MasterCard ☐ Call me for credit information - Phone _____

Card # _____ Exp. Date _____

Signature _____

Name _____

Address _____

City _____ State _____ Zip _____